ADAPTED TO SURVIVE

ANIMALS THAT CLIMB

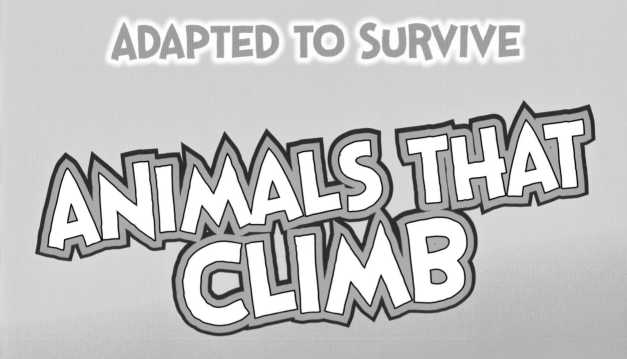

Angela Royston

 Raintree

Chicago, Illinois

© 2014 Raintree
an imprint of Capstone Global Library, LLC
Chicago, Illinois

To contact Capstone Global Library please
phone 800-747-4992, or visit our web site,
www.capstonepub.com

All rights reserved. No part of this publication may
be reproduced or transmitted in any form or by
any means, electronic or mechanical, including
photocopying, recording, taping, or any information
storage and retrieval system, without permission in
writing from the publisher.

Edited by Dan Nunn, Rebecca Rissman, and Helen
Cox Cannons
Designed by Jo Hinton-Malivoire
Picture research by Mica Brancic
Production by Helen McCreath
Originated by Capstone Global Library Ltd
Printed and bound in China

17 16 15 14 13
10 9 8 7 6 5 4 3 2 1

**Library of Congress Cataloging-in-Publication
Data**
Royston, Angela, 1945- author.
  Animals that climb / Angela Royston.
    pages cm.—(Adapted to survive)
  Includes bibliographical references and index.
  ISBN 978-1-4109-6148-8 (hb)—ISBN 978-1-4109-
6155-6 (pb) 1. Animal climbing—Juvenile literature.
2. Animals—Adaptation—Juvenile literature. I. Title.

QL751.5.R693 2014
591.5—dc23   2013017632

Acknowledgments
The author and publisher are grateful to the
following for permission to reproduce copyright
material: FLPA pp. 19 (Minden Pictures/Thomas
Marent), 26 (Minden Pictures/Pete Oxford); Getty
Images p. 18 (AFP Photo/Alfredo Estrella); Naturepl.
com pp. 5 (© Eric Baccega), 6 (© Yukihiro Fukuda),
8 (© Kevin Schafer), 9 (ARCO/© Reinhard), 10,
24 (© Ingo Arndt), 11 (© Nature Production), 12
(2020VISION/© Peter Cairns), 14 (© Jouan & Rius),
15 (© Steven David Miller), 16 (© Andy Rouse), 17
(© Angela Scott), 23 (© Nick Garbutt); Science
Photo Library p. 27 (Power and Syred); Shutterstock
pp. 4 (© Redwood), 7 (© Irina Mos), 29 top left (©
Foxtrot101), 29 bottom left (© Florence McGinn), 29
bottom right (© Eric Isselee), 29 top right (© Martin
Lehmann); SuperStock pp. 13 (Prisma), 20 (Minden
Pictures), 21 (Biosphoto), 22 (F1 ONLINE), 25 (age
fotostock).

Cover photograph of a Victorian koala in a
Eucalyptus tree, Adelaide, Australia, reproduced
with permission of Shutterstock (© Cloudia
Newland).

We would like to thank Michael Bright for his
invaluable help in the preparation of this book.

Every effort has been made to contact copyright
holders of any material reproduced in this book.
Any omissions will be rectified in subsequent
printings if notice is given to the publisher.

All the Internet addresses (URLs) given in this
book were valid at the time of going to press.
However, due to the dynamic nature of the
Internet, some addresses may have changed,
or sites may have changed or ceased to exist
since publication. While the author and publisher
regret any inconvenience this may cause readers,
no responsibility for any such changes can be
accepted by either the author or the publisher.

Some words are shown in bold, **like this**. You can find
out what they mean by looking in the glossary.

CONTENTS

Good at Climbing 4

Climbing to Survive 6

Adapted to Climb 8

Mountain Goats 10

Squirrels .12

Koalas 14

Leopards 16

Spider Monkeys 18

Handy Tails 20

Tree Snakes 22

Geckos 24

Tree Frogs 26

Animal Challenge 28

Glossary .30

Find Out More 31

Index 32

GOOD AT CLIMBING

Many different types of animals are good at climbing. For example, squirrels climb up trees and poles, and lizards scamper up steep rocks. Good climbers may be large or small.

Pandas are very good at climbing. But what makes them such good climbers?

CLIMBING TO SURVIVE

Climbing helps animals **survive**. Being able to climb allows some animals to escape from danger and to find food in places other animals cannot reach.

A monkey can pick fruit from the top of a tree.

Bighorn sheep live high in the mountains. Their **hooves** grip the steep rocks. They move so fast that they can usually escape from mountain lions, who hunt them.

ADAPTED TO CLIMB

Adaptations are special things about an animal's body that help it **survive**. Animals have **adapted** to climbing in different ways. For example, many tree climbers have sharp claws and strong legs.

three-toed sloth

two-toed sloth

DID YOU KNOW?
Sloths spend most of their lives hanging upside down in trees!

MOUNTAIN GOATS

Mountain goats are well **adapted** for living on steep mountainsides. They can spread and squeeze their **hooves**, so their rough **pads** are able to grip the smallest footholds. When a **predator** comes, the goats quickly find a safe ledge.

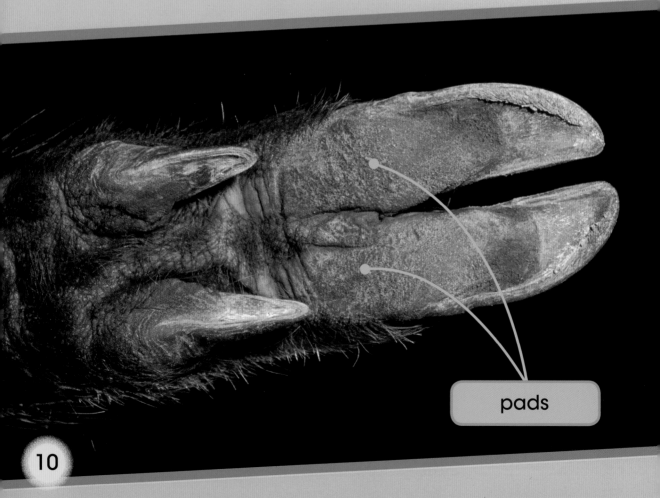

pads

Born Climbers

Baby mountain goats begin to run and jump when they are just a few hours old.

SQUIRRELS

A squirrel is a champion tree climber. It spreads its sharp claws to grip the tree. Its bushy tail helps it steer as it jumps from tree to tree. Squirrels are so light that they can climb along the thinnest branches to reach nuts to eat.

Squirrels hold on tightly
when a branch bends.

KOALAS

Koalas are well **adapted** to climbing trees. They have strong leg **muscles**, sharp claws, and rough **pads** on their paws to grip the bark. A koala is a **marsupial**. A marsupial mother carries her baby in her pouch.

Climbing Kangaroo
Tree kangaroos are also marsupials that climb trees! They live high up in tropical forests.

LEOPARDS

Unlike most big cats, a leopard is at home in the trees. It grips the tree with its big feet and claws, and uses its long tail to balance. When a leopard kills an antelope, it eats some of it and hides the rest for later. Sometimes the leopard drags the **carcass** up a tree.

A leopard can sleep on the branch of a tree.

SPIDER MONKEYS

Spider monkeys live in South American rain forests. They have long arms and a long tail, which they use like an extra arm to grip the trees. A patch of bare skin at the end of their tail helps them grip things.

HANDY TAILS

A tail that can grip is called a **prehensile tail**. Spider monkeys are not the only animals that have them. Chameleons and harvest mice have them, too. Harvest mice live in wheat fields and among tall grasses. They use their wide feet and long prehensile tail to help them climb from stalk to stalk.

chameleon

harvest mouse

TREE SNAKES

Tree snakes have long, thin bodies. A tree snake has no legs, so it grips the tree with its body. Tree snakes move easily from branch to branch. They also wind themselves around a branch to rest in the sunshine or wait for **prey**.

This green tree snake lives in forests in northern Australia.

Prehensile Body
A tree snake uses its whole body like a **prehensile tail!**

GECKOS

A gecko lizard is an amazing climber. It has a **pad** at the end of each toe. The pad is covered with tiny, flat bristles that stick to most surfaces. A gecko can even walk across the ceiling to catch insects!

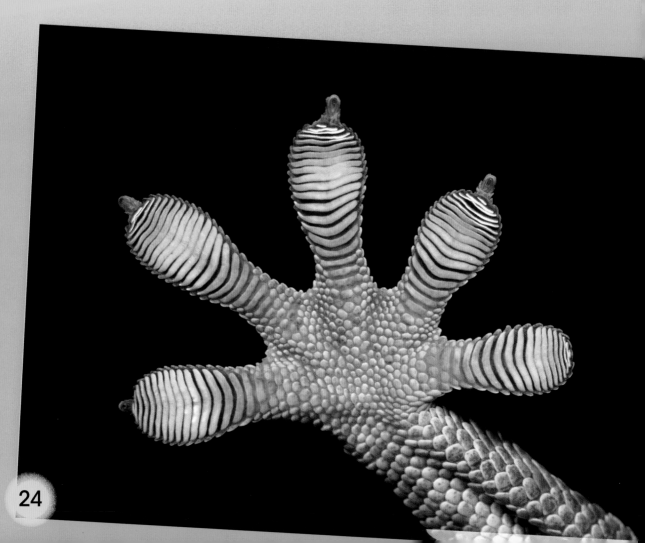

Smart Move!
When the gecko wants to unstick its feet, it just curls up its toes.

TREE FROGS

A tree frog spends most of its life in trees. It hops from leaf to leaf on its long back legs. Each toe has a large, round **pad**. The pads are wet and stick to the leaves. They allow the frog to move safely.

A fly has hairy pads under its feet. The hairs make their own sticky glue!

hairy pads

ANIMAL CHALLENGE

1. Why can't a mountain goat climb tall trees?

2. What **adaptations** does a pet cat have to help it climb trees?

3. Which do you think can climb trees better— a gorilla or a dog?

Invent a new climbing animal! Think about where your animal will climb and why. You can use some of the adaptations shown in the photos, or make up your own.

claws

long tail

strong legs

sticky **pads**

Answers to Animal Challenge

1. An animal needs sharp claws to climb trees, but a goat has smooth, rounded **hooves**.
2. Cats have sharp claws for clinging to the bark. Their long tails help them balance on the branches.
3. A gorilla has fingers and toes that grip rough bark and branches. A dog's claws are not sharp enough to dig into the bark.

GLOSSARY

adaptation special thing about an animal's body that helps it survive in a particular way or in a particular habitat

adapted well suited to a particular activity or way of living

carcass dead body of an animal

hooves hard covers that protect the feet of some animals, such as goats and horses

marsupial animal that carries its newborn baby in a pouch on the mother's body

muscle fleshy part of the body that makes a particular part of the body move

pad soft, tough cushion under the feet of many animals

predator animal that hunts and kills other animals for food

prehensile tail tail that is able to grip or hold onto something

prey animal that is hunted and eaten by another animal

survive manage to go on living

FIND OUT MORE

BOOKS

Amstutz, Lisa J. *Rain Forest Animal Adaptations.* Mankato, Minn.: Capstone, 2012.

Gosman, Gillian. *Spider Monkeys.* New York: Rosen, 2012.

Kolpin, Molly. *Giant Pandas.* Mankato, Minn.: Capstone, 2012.

Robbins, Lynette. *Tree Frogs* (Jump!). New York: Rosen, 2012.

WEB SITES

FactHound offers a safe, fun way to find Internet sites related to this book. All of the sites on FactHound have been researched by our staff.

Here's all you do:
Visit www.facthound.com
Type in this code: 9781410961488

INDEX

adaptations 8, 30
adapted 8, 10, 14, 30

balance 16, 29
bighorn sheep 7

carcasses 16, 30
cats 28, 29
chameleons 20
claws 12, 14, 16, 29

dogs 28, 29

escape 6, 7

flies 27
food, finding 6, 12

geckos 24-25
gorillas 28, 29

harvest mice 20, 21
hooves 7, 10, 30

koalas 14

leopards 16-17
lizards 4, 24-25

marsupials 14, 30
monkeys 6, 18-19, 20
mountain goats 10-11,
  28, 29
mountains 7, 10
muscles 14, 30

pads 10, 14, 24, 26, 27, 30
pandas 5
pouches 14
predators 10, 30
prehensile tails 20, 23, 30
prey 22, 30

sloths 8-9
spider monkeys 18-19, 20
squirrels 4, 12-13
steer 12
survive 6-7, 8, 30

tails 12, 16, 18, 20, 23, 29
tree climbers 8, 12
tree frogs 26
tree kangaroos 15
tree snakes 22-23

31192020571889